W9-DFF-319

PLAY BETTER GOLF

CURING HOOKS AND SLICES

Straighten the curving shots

Beverly Lewis

Illustrations by Ken Lewis

SMITHMARK

CLB 3150
© 1991 CLB Publishing,

This edition published in 1994 by
SMITHMARK Publishers, Inc.,
16 East 32nd Street, New York, NY 10016

SMITHMARK books are available for bulk purchase for sales
promotion and premium use. For details write or call the
manager of special sales, SMITHMARK Publishers, Inc.,
16 East 32nd Street, New York, NY 10016; (212) 532-6600.

Produced by CLB Publishing,
Godalming Business Centre, Woolsack Way,
Godalming, Surrey GU7 1XW

ISBN 0-8317-4039-6

Printed and bound in Malaysia
10 9 8 7 6 5 4 3 2 1

Contents

Beverly and Ken Lewis

Beverly Lewis became a professional golfer in 1978 and has twice been Chairman of the Women's Professional Golf Association. A PGA qualified professional since 1982, she has played in many major tournaments and is an experienced teacher. She has been a regular contributor to *Golf World* magazine in the United Kingdom for six years and is the only woman on their teaching panel. She has won two tournaments on the WPGA circuit but now concentrates on her teaching commitments.

Beverly is co-author of *Improve Your Golf* (published in the UK by Collins Willow, revised edition), and has written the other titles in the *Golf Clinic Series*. Her interests include music and playing the organ.

Ken Lewis trained at the Southend College of Art and then worked as a commercial artist. He has illustrated many golf books, working with players such as Peter Alliss, Alex Hay and Sandy Lyle. His projects include illustrating newspaper instructional features and strips by Greg Norman and Nick Faldo, and he works for *Golf* Magazine in the United States. His hobbies include building and flying his own aeroplane.

CHAPTER ONE

Hitting curving shots is easy

Of all the sports so far invented, golf has to be one of the most exacting when it comes to tolerance of error. Looking at it in an objective manner, you expect to hit an object — the golf ball, which has a diameter of under two inches — with another object — the golf club, on which the ideal and most efficient area of strike, the sweet spot, is nearer one inch in diameter. You swing this club something like twenty feet through a backswing and downswing before you strike the ball and, in order to hit a shot that does not deviate from its intended target, the club must be swinging down the correct path, and the club face must be positioned squarely and approaching from the optimum angle. If you are slightly adrift in any of these requirements, you will hit a shot that curves either slightly or violently, depending on your degree of error.

I also believe that it is a far from natural game, and most aspects have to be learnt rather than coming from some marvellous innate sixth sense. Admittedly, there are those people who take to the game in what seems to be a very natural way, but they are few and far between and are the sort who would excel in any sport. They not only have superb hand and eye co-ordination but also the ability to copy the correct action. Therefore, provided that they have seen the best golfers play (and with so much television coverage of the sport these days, that is almost inevitable) they will most likely swing the club in a respectable manner. However, to progress and to make the most of their talent, they too would need lessons in order to be guided along the correct lines so that they do not start to fall into bad habits. For the rest of humanity, their first attempts at golf will result inevitably in plenty of mis-hits and shots that veer from the straight and narrow. This is only to be expected since the good golf shot requires the correct swing path, club face alignment and angle of attack.

I believe that if you have a good idea and mental picture of what you should be doing and how the club should be swinging, then you have a better chance of producing that swing. This book aims to give you a working knowledge of the geometry of the swing, why certain shots are hit, and what you can do to straighten those shots.

CHAPTER TWO

The geometry of golf shots

Before deciding what your swing problems might be and how best to cure them, it is important that you are armed with the knowledge to analyse your swing. The best aid for this is to examine the flight characteristics of the ball, thereby revealing the two major factors that affect the shot, i.e. the direction of the swing path and club face alignment. Although your shots may not even have a regular pattern to them, it is more than likely that there are some things that you repeat quite often, perhaps at this stage unknown to you. However, by adding to your knowledge of the ball flight laws, you will make some discoveries about your swing that should help you become more consistent.

The in-to-in swing

In order to give you a good picture of what should happen

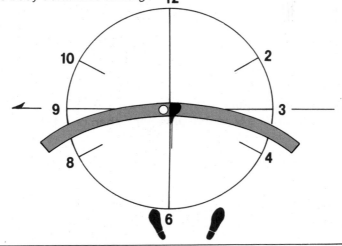

Fig 2.1. This shows the correct in-to-in swing path where the club head swings back between 3 and 4 o'clock, returns on a similar path, striking the ball whilst moving towards 9 o'clock, then swings back inside towards 8 o'clock as the body continues turning

in the swing, I like to use the clock face as a guide. Imagine that the ball is in the centre of a clock and that you are standing at 6 o'clock with 3 o'clock on your right and 9 o'clock on your left. As the club head moves away from the ball, initially it swings towards 3 o'clock. Then, as the body continues turning, it is swung inwards and upwards between 3 and 4 o'clock. It is swung down virtually on the same path, strikes the ball while it is moving towards 9 o'clock and then, as the body continues turning, swings inside towards 8 o'clock (Fig 2.1). This ideal swing path is known as in-to-in, so called because the club head approaches the ball from inside an imaginary line through the ball to the target (in this case represented by 3 to 9 o'clock) and then, having hit the ball, swings back inside this line.

Club face alignment

Even with the correct in-to-in swing path, if the ball is to go straight then the club face must be square to the swing path at impact (Fig 2.2a). The club head can be facing in one of three directions at impact:

Square — facing the same direction as the swing path;
Open — facing right of the swing path;
Closed — facing left of the swing path.

If the swing path is in-to-in but the club face is open at impact, the ball will start straight and then curve to the right near the end of its flight (Fig 2.2b).

If the swing path is in-to-in but the club face is closed at impact, the ball will start straight and then curve to the left near the end of its flight (Fig 2.2c).

The ball's initial direction is governed mainly by the path of the club head; then, as it nears the end of its flight, any sidespin imparted by the club face causes it to curve in the direction of the spin.

If the club face is square at impact, then only backspin affects the ball and it will fly straight throughout its journey. If the club face is open at impact, left to right spin will be imparted on the ball, and that is why it will curve in that direction towards the end of its flight.

If the club face is closed at impact, right to left spin will be imparted on the ball, and that is why it will spin in that direction towards the end of its flight.

The more the club face is open or closed at impact, the

Fig 2.2. With the correct in-to-in path, the ball starts straight but the flight varies according to club face alignment at impact:

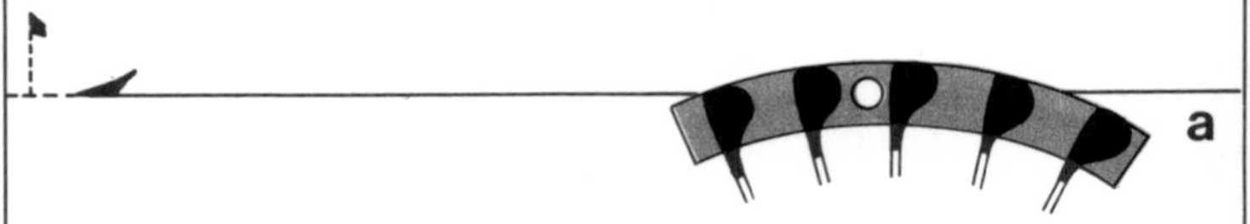

(a) club face square, ball goes straight

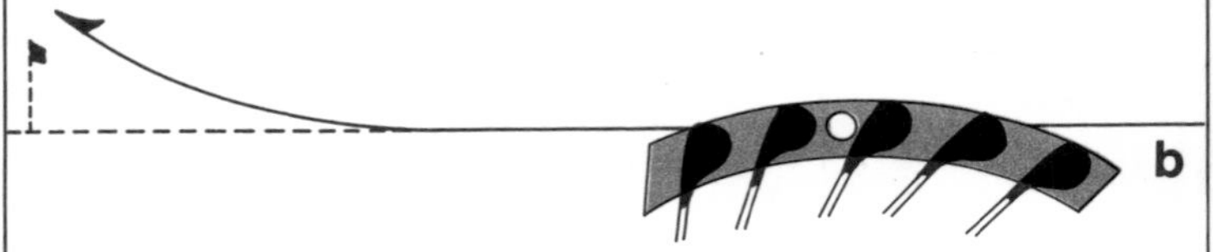

(b) club face open, curves to the right

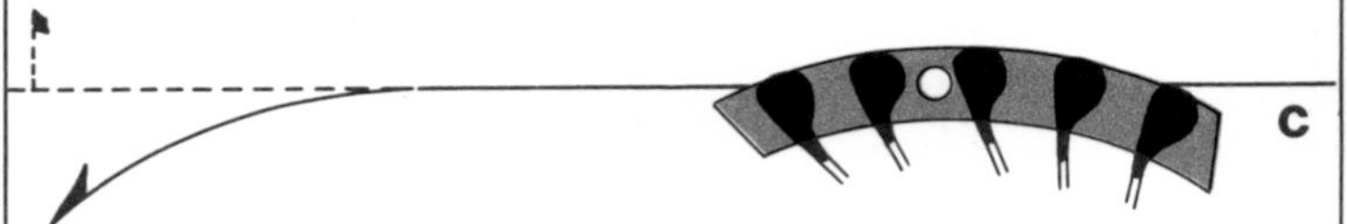

(c) club face closed, ball curves to the left

greater the curve in flight. Furthermore, if the club face is in either of these extreme positions, it will influence the initial direction of the ball. Usually the beginner who has trouble squaring the club face will be able to produce a great variety of shots from what may appear to be the same swing. What is happening is that the club face may be wide open on one shot, sending the ball immediately to the right on a high trajectory, and then very closed on the next shot, making the ball fly immediately left and very low. Although the club may have been swung in the same direction, the extremely open or closed club face alignment has become the greater influence on the shot so that the ball will start in the direction to which the club face was looking, rather than the direction in which it was swinging. Thus many beginners find it difficult to analyse their shots. However, most players tend to swing the club in the same direction but prove to be inconsistent with club face alignment.

It is also indisputable that the more lofted clubs do not impart as much sidespin as the straighter faced clubs. The reason for this is that the less lofted clubs contact the ball nearer to its equator and usually at a shallower angle of attack, thereby imparting more sidespin than backspin, and it is the sidespin that causes the ball to curve in the air (Fig 2.3a). A more lofted club contacts the ball lower

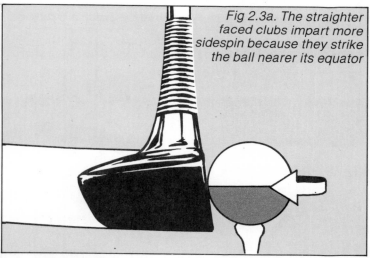

Fig 2.3a. The straighter faced clubs impart more sidespin because they strike the ball nearer its equator

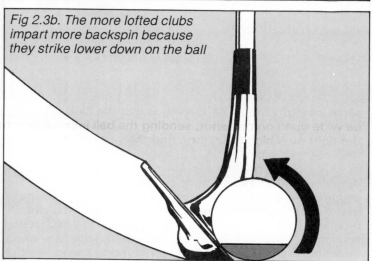

Fig 2.3b. The more lofted clubs impart more backspin because they strike lower down on the ball

down, and usually at a fairly steep angle of attack, thus creating maximum backspin and minimum sidespin (Fig 2.3b). In this instance, backspin becomes more influential than sidespin, and the result is a shot that does not curve too much in the air although it may not always be struck in the direction of the target.

The out-to-in swing path

Whenever the club head approaches the ball from outside

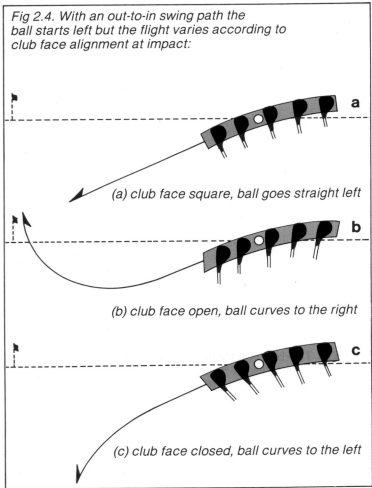

Fig 2.4. With an out-to-in swing path the ball starts left but the flight varies according to club face alignment at impact:

(a) club face square, ball goes straight left

(b) club face open, ball curves to the right

(c) club face closed, ball curves to the left

the imaginary line through the ball to the target, it is called an out-to-in swing path and will cause the ball to start left of the target. To use the clock face analogy, the club head is swinging more along a line in the 2 to 8 o'clock direction although, of course, the out-to-in symptom may not be as extreme as this. However, as with the in-to-in swing, the club face can be in one of three positions at impact — square, open or closed — and each will affect the shot differently.

If the swing path is out-to-in, with the club face square at impact, the ball will start left and continue straight left (Fig 2.4a).

If the swing path is out-to-in, with the club face open at impact, the ball will start left and then curve to the right (Fig 2.4b). The ball will fly higher than normal.

If the swing path is out-to-in, with the club face closed, the ball will start left and then curve left (Fig 2.4c). The ball will fly lower than normal.

The in-to-out swing path

Whenever the club head approaches the ball from inside the ball to target line and then swings to the outside of that line, it is known as an in-to-out swing and will cause the ball to start to the right of the target. Again, using the clock face as a comparison, the club head will be swinging more from the direction of 4 to 10 o'clock, although the swing may not necessarily be as extreme as this. As with the two previous examples, the club face can be square, open or closed.

If the swing path is in-to-out, with the club face square at impact, the ball starts right and continues straight right (Fig 2.5a).

If the swing path is in-to-out, with the club face open at impact, the ball starts right and then curves to the right (Fig 2.5b). The ball will fly higher than normal.

If the swing path is in-to-out, with the club face closed at impact, the ball starts right and then curves to the left (Fig 2.5c). The ball will fly lower than normal.

From these explanations of the geometry of the swing, you can see that three different swing paths are possible as are three different club face alignments. Any combination will give one of the flight characteristics detailed above, and your shots will fall into one or maybe more of these categories. However, there is another factor

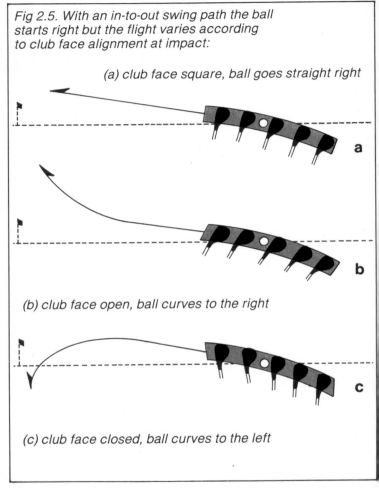

Fig 2.5. With an in-to-out swing path the ball starts right but the flight varies according to club face alignment at impact:

(a) club face square, ball goes straight right

a

(b) club face open, ball curves to the right

b

(c) club face closed, ball curves to the left

c

that affects the ball's flight and that is the angle of attack.

Angle of attack

As you address the ball, you stand to the side of it rather than directly above it, and thus the correct club head path should be from in-to-in. Because the ball is on the ground and not sitting on a tee at eye level, you must also have an up and down element in the swing. In golfing terms, this is known as the angle of attack. As the club head approaches impact it swings downward and then parallel to the ground before starting to swing upwards. Therefore, you have the opportunity to hit the ball when the club head is travelling at one of three angles: downward, level or upward. Different shots call for different angles of approach.

Different swing paths create and affect the angle of attack. The correct in-to-in swing path provides an angle that is the most suitable for all shots, and in order to create a downward angle for the irons, through to a slightly upward angle for the driver, adjustment is made to the ball position, width of stance and weight distribution. The angle of attack will then become correct automatically for the type of strike required.

An out-to-in swing will create a steep attack on the ball, which tends to concentrate too much force downwards and insufficient forwards and thereby distance is lost. A player in this category will take quite deep divots which will point well left of the target (Fig 2.6a) and will be happier hitting irons, preferably short ones, rather than woods. The steepness of attack will promote backspin, sending the ball higher than it should go, and since this line of swing is more usually accompanied by an open club face (which adds loft to the club), all shots lack their true potential in distance. Whereas the steepness of attack can be tolerated to some degree with the irons, when it comes to woods, and especially woods teed up, the angle of attack is a considerable drawback. It is likely that tee shots will be hit with the top of the face, resulting in a skied shot (Fig 2.6b) whereas the best result will be a shot lacking in length.

The in-to-out swing path creates a shallow attack on the ball and will thus emphasize the forward motion in the swing, yielding good distance but making a consistent solid strike with iron shots rather more difficult and unlikely. Because the angle of attack is shallow, it is easy to hit behind the ball since the base of the arc often occurs before the ball is struck (Fig 2.6c). Players in this category will enjoy hitting a ball teed up or from a very good lie rather than from a bare lie. Since the swing lacks the correct downward approach, less backspin is imparted and so the shots tend to fly lower than normal and can thereby produce more length.

Summary

These golfing facts will help you to understand how you swing and to appreciate into which category you fit. Most golfers tend to be consistent in the direction in which they swing the club, i.e. the swing path, but less so in getting the club face in the same position at impact, thus leading to shots that go in totally different directions. At first you will not necessarily remember or even understand the explanations of the factors that affect the ball's flight, so take some time to re-read this chapter and refer back to it when necessary.

Try to remember that it is the direction in which the club head is swinging, i.e. the swing path, that is the greatest influence on the initial direction of the ball. Club face alignment will also affect the initial direction of the shot to some extent but will only be of great significance, perhaps over-riding the swing path direction, if extremely open or closed. Club face alignment is responsible for imparting spin which will make the ball curve towards the end of its flight. The angle of attack and club head speed will influence further the height and distance of the shot.

For those of you who have no knowledge of the golf swing and look upon it as one of life's mysteries, I can assure you that by the end of this book you will have learnt a lot, hopefully sufficient to be able to improve considerably.

Fig 2.6a. An out-to-in swing path creates a steep angle of attack which means that the player will take deep divots that point left of target

Fig 2.6b. A steep angle of attack can lead to tee shots being struck with the top of the club face

Fig. 2.6c. The shallow angle of attack from an in-to-out swing path can cause the base of the arc to fall before the ball, making it difficult to consistently hit crisp iron shots

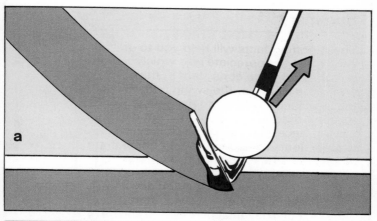

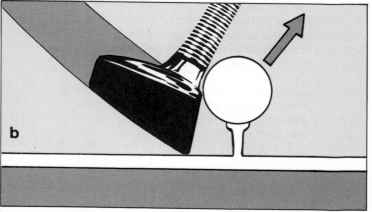

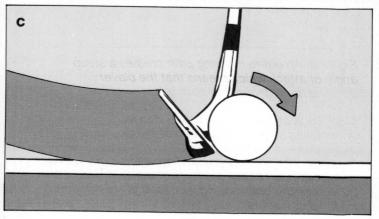

CHAPTER THREE

Why more golfers slice than hook

You learnt in Chapter 2 that the alignment of the club face at impact is one of the greatest variables in golf, causing the beginner and higher handicap player to hit a wide variety of shots. The correct hand action has to be learnt so that the club face is returned at least reasonably square to the in-to-in swing path at impact, resulting in a shot with little curve to the ball flight. Unfortunately, the correct hand and arm action is not natural to beginners, and generally their version of swinging a club usually returns the club face open at impact, resulting in a shot that curves to the right.

For a start, many people grip the club incorrectly and inevitably have trouble returning the club face squarely to the ball. Many players also grip too tightly, fearing that if they do not do so they will have insufficient control and the club may slip in their hands. Gripping too tightly definitely stifles hand and wrist action so that they lack the freedom of movement necessary if the hands, wrists and arms are to contribute fully to the shot (Fig 3.1). Instead, you are more likely to see a person swinging in a stiff manner — trying to use sheer force to propel the ball forward. In fact, describing a beginner's action as a 'swing' is, in most cases, far from the truth because swing is the one factor that is missing from their action. They lack the freedom to swing their hands and arms which, in turn, will swing the club head, and consequently the clubface is left open at impact sending the ball to the right. Thus it seems only logical to aim to the left to allow for it. But this action aligns the body so that the swing path of the club is out-to-in in relation to the target, and the ball's flight will now be influenced not only by an open clubface but by an out-to-in swing path, both of which will impart slicing sidespin. In this way, the error is compounded.

There is another classic cause of slicing which stems mainly from bad alignment. Aiming the swing and yourself in the correct direction is not the easiest aspect of golf and is often neglected by the beginner. In many instances, a pupil aims a long way right of the target, and then the only way to get the swing back on track is to develop a loop to the outside at the start of the downswing. This action feels quite natural since it involves using the powerful muscles in the right shoulder area, and for most beginners, at the top of the swing, this area feels most able to deliver a solid blow to the ball. But the shoulder and back muscles are big and slow and cannot produce enough club head speed to hit the ball a long way. The looping action again sets the swing across the ball from out-to-in and with good hand action missing, once again you have the blueprint for a slice.

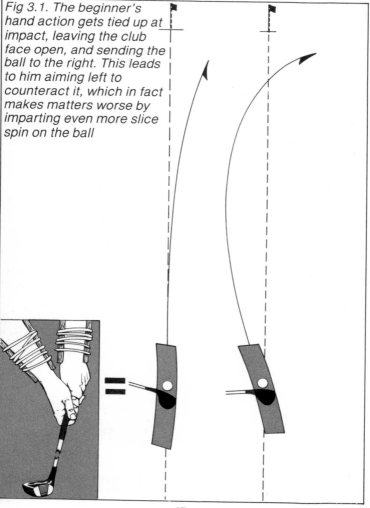

Fig 3.1. The beginner's hand action gets tied up at impact, leaving the club face open, and sending the ball to the right. This leads to him aiming left to counteract it, which in fact makes matters worse by imparting even more slice spin on the ball

CHAPTER FOUR

The correct grip

The purpose of the grip is to return the club face squarely to the ball without any undue or independent manipulation of the hands. The technique of the game of golf has evolved over many years, matching the evolution of the equipment used, and whereas fifty years ago players may have had to employ a hand action that facilitated the hickory shafts of their era, today's

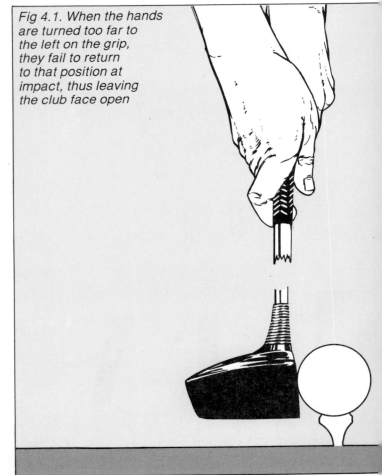

Fig 4.1. When the hands are turned too far to the left on the grip, they fail to return to that position at impact, thus leaving the club face open

equipment allows a simpler method of playing golf and one that advocates quite simple hand action. However, without first gripping the club correctly, the hands are unable to work either in the right direction or in harmony and this is how problems may begin.

Each of us may have hands that work at different speeds; certainly those people who use their hands quite actively at work will have developed strong muscles and consequently will be able to derive a great deal of power from them. But the power will lie dormant or be destructive if the grip is technically suspect and does not naturally return the club face square at impact.

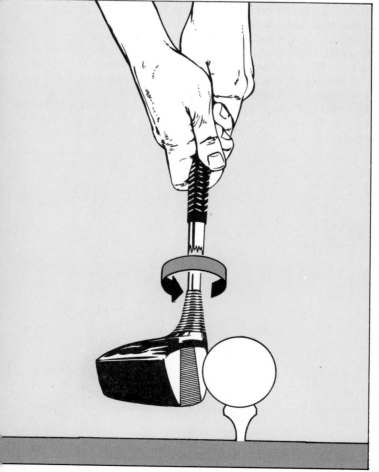

Constructing the grip

The slicer is usually born as a result of poor hand action, which usually results from placing the hands on the grip incorrectly, with either one or both hands turned too much to the left so that the 'V's formed by the thumb and forefinger point too much towards the chin or left ear. At impact, the hands fail to return to their address position and instead are facing more to the right. Of course, the club face matches this change and it too faces right of the target (Fig 4.1).

To correct this, place the left hand on the grip with the shaft across the palm of the hand and the end of the grip under the fleshy pad at the heel of the hand and cradled in the forefinger (Fig 4.2). Close the last three fingers round the grip, and make certain that when you look down you can see at least two to two-and-a-half knuckles (Fig 4.3). The thumb should sit just to the right of centre of the front of the grip, and there should not be a large gap between the base of the thumb and the forefinger, since this part of the hand must provide much of the support at the top of the swing. You may find it easier to check if the grip

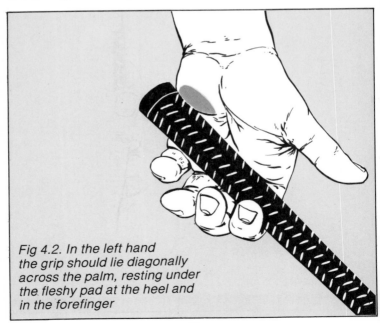

Fig 4.2. In the left hand the grip should lie diagonally across the palm, resting under the fleshy pad at the heel and in the forefinger

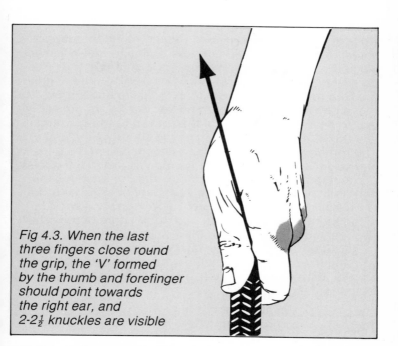

Fig 4.3. When the last three fingers close round the grip, the 'V' formed by the thumb and forefinger should point towards the right ear, and 2-2½ knuckles are visible

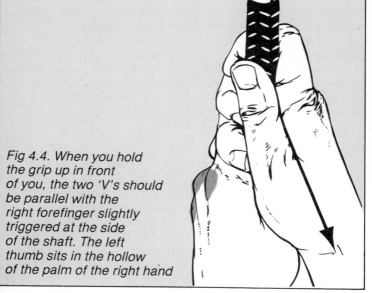

Fig 4.4. When you hold the grip up in front of you, the two 'V's should be parallel with the right forefinger slightly triggered at the side of the shaft. The left thumb sits in the hollow of the palm of the right hand

conforms to these standards by holding the club up in front of you. The 'V' between the thumb and forefinger should point in the region of your right ear, and when you place the right hand on the grip make sure that the 'V' is parallel to the left hand 'V' (Fig 4.4). The right hand grips the club more in the fingers than the palm and fingers, so that it can provide maximum power. Again, do not allow a gap to develop between the thumb and forefinger, and rest the thumb just to the left of the centre of the grip. The forefinger should feel slightly triggered on the grip and you will find that the left thumb will rest in the hollow of the right hand. Whether you overlap, or interlock the right little finger, or even grip with ten fingers on the club, is a matter of personal preference. Personally, I would recommend the overlapping grip but if either of the other two feel more comfortable, then so be it.

Placed on the club in this fashion, you will find that if you uncurl your fingers, then the hands are practically parallel, with the back of the left and palm of the right facing the target.

The very strong grip

It is also possible to slice with a very strong grip, i.e. both hands are turned well to the right so that you can see three or four knuckles on your left hand (Fig 4.5). What happens with this type of grip is that the hands are blocked through impact with the heel of the left hand going towards the target. If the hands were to release you would hook the ball quite viciously since they are in such a strong position. You need to adjust the grip to suit the recommendations above by moving both hands round to the left.

Grip pressure

Grip pressure is applied by the last three fingers of the left hand and the middle two of the right, and should be light rather than tight. It is difficult to be exact about grip pressure but you are gripping too tightly if the muscles in your forearms feel hard and taut. For muscles to work most efficiently, they must be relaxed and soft. Grip the club in your left hand only and place your right hand on your left forearm. By increasing the left-hand grip pressure you will feel the muscles tighten and harden. Now slacken the pressure until they feel relaxed and you will be nearer the correct grip pressure.

At this stage, the new grip will feel far from comfortable since any change of grip feels extremely awkward initially but the sooner you decide to commit yourself to this change, then the sooner and quicker you will progress. Try to practise the grip for at least 5 to 10 minutes a day so that you quickly get used to the unaccustomed position.

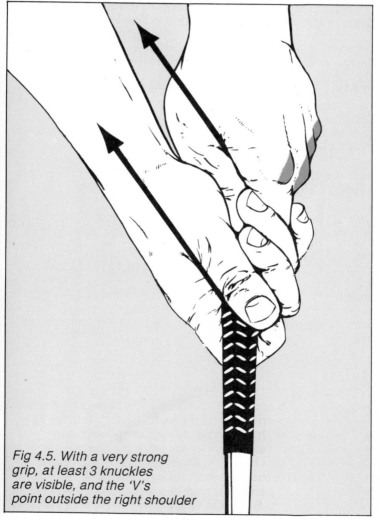

Fig 4.5. With a very strong grip, at least 3 knuckles are visible, and the 'V's point outside the right shoulder

CHAPTER FIVE

Correcting the set up

As a natural reaction to the ball curving to the right, many players who slice start to aim left. When you address the ball, ideally you should try to set yourself parallel to an imaginary line between the ball and target. This will then enable you to swing the club head on the correct in-to-in path. In clock face terms, the ball to target line is from 3 o'clock to 9 o'clock, and you stand parallel to that (Fig 2.1). However, the slicing golfer who aligns his or her body much more along the 2 o'clock to 8 o'clock line, consequently swings from out-to-in.

The golfer who aims a long way to the right sets the body more along a line in the 4 o'clock to 10 o'clock direction, but then inserts a looping action into the swing so that the club head inevitably approaches more from the 2 o'clock direction (Fig 5.1).

Intermediate target

One of the easiest ways to set up correctly is to use an intermediate target, which is approximately three feet

Fig 5.1. The golfer who aims a long way right, tends to loop his swing onto an outside path in the downswing

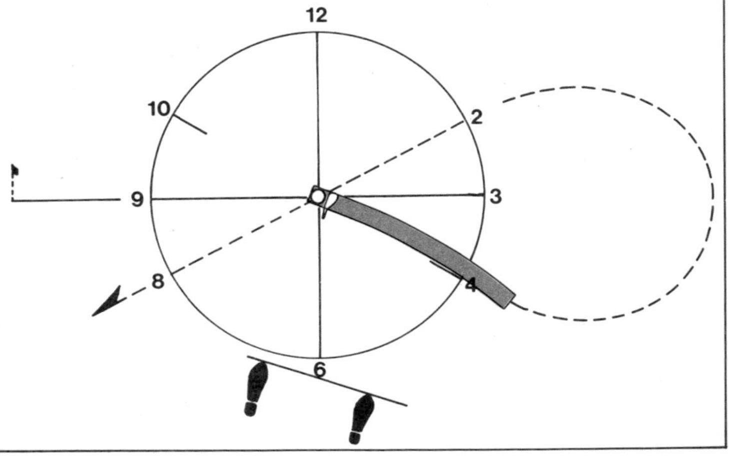

Fig 5.2. The golfer on the left shows the ideal set up to slice, with the shoulders open. To counteract this use an intermediate target to aim over, and a slightly closed shoulder and eye line to encourage an inside takeway

In order to have a good mental image of the set up, liken it to a railway track where the ball and clubhead are on the far rail, and you stand on the near one

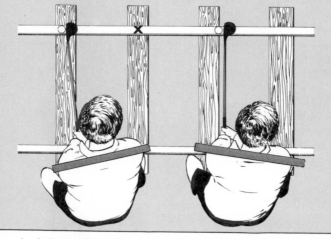

ahead of the ball on the target line. So standing behind the ball and looking towards the target, pick out a divot or leaf just ahead of the ball. Then standing opposite the ball, place the club head behind the ball square to this imaginary line and the target. At this stage of your progress, it would be useful either to place two clubs down, one just outside the ball and the other about 18 inches nearer to you and parallel to the target, or to work on your set up standing on square patio slabs or kitchen floor tiles where the straight lines will help considerably. The new address position will feel strange initially, and any endorsement you can get to assure you that you are now square to the target and not aiming miles to the right or left will enhance your progress and belief in what you are doing.

It is important for you to check first that the club face is square. It is often difficult for the player to appreciate that the blade may be misaligned, but with the help of clubs on the ground, or the square tiles, this should become obvious.

Next position your feet, knees and hips parallel to the ball to target line. The most important parts of the body in determining the swing path are the shoulders, and ideally these too should be parallel, but since you are trying to cure an out-to-in swing path, it would be beneficial at this stage to align your shoulders a little closed, so that a club placed across them would point more towards the target than parallel to it. This over-correction will help you to keep the club on an inside path, and when that becomes more automatic you can consider re-aligning the shoulders back to the parallel position. However, I must stress that

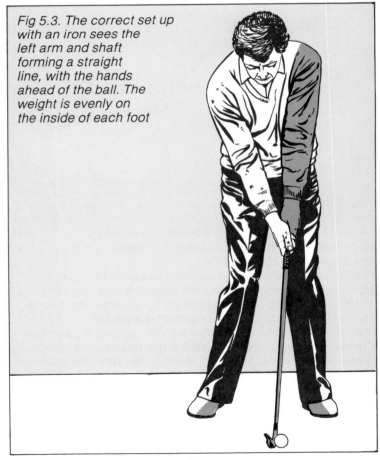

Fig 5.3. The correct set up with an iron sees the left arm and shaft forming a straight line, with the hands ahead of the ball. The weight is evenly on the inside of each foot

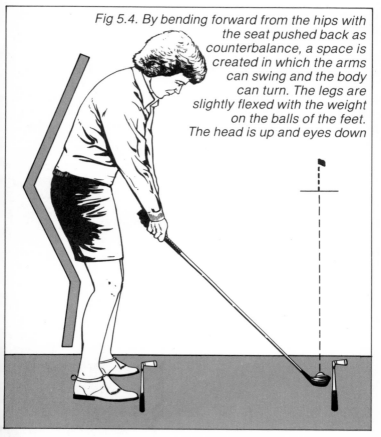

Fig 5.4. By bending forward from the hips with the seat pushed back as counterbalance, a space is created in which the arms can swing and the body can turn. The legs are slightly flexed with the weight on the balls of the feet. The head is up and eyes down

the shoulders should be only slightly closed and not aimed a long way right (Fig 5.2).

As a similar aid to encouraging the correct inside backswing path, and also to visualizing it, set your eye-line so that a club held across your eyes and under the bridge of your nose would aim just right of the parallel.

Most golfers who slice have trouble making a good turn in the backswing, and so to make this easier, angle your right foot out about 15 to 20° at address, but make sure that the left foot is fairly square to the line of flight, or only just turned out.

Whereas the left arm is straight at address, the right arm should feel soft to enable it to fold easily on the backswing, so allow it to bend very slightly, with the elbow pointing towards the right hip bone. Check your set up in a mirror, and when viewed face on your left arm and the shaft should form a straight line. The shaft must slope towards the target so that your hands are ahead of the ball (Fig 5.3). Many golfers who slice, start with their hands behind the ball with the left wrist kinked inwards, which leads to a hands and arms only backswing with no shoulder turn. By setting up correctly, you have a much better chance of a good shoulder turn.

If you stand with the mirror to your right, you should just be able to see your left shoulder in it, which will indicate that the shoulders are slightly closed.

In order to have a good mental image of the set up, liken it to railway lines, where the ball and club head are on the far rail and you stand on the near one (Fig 5.2).

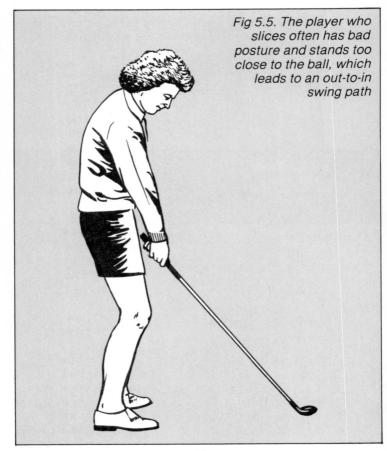

Fig 5.5. The player who slices often has bad posture and stands too close to the ball, which leads to an out-to-in swing path

Good posture

In order that your body and arms can work correctly
throughout the swing, good posture is essential.
Therefore you must bend forward from the hips to create
a space in front of you in which your arms can swing. At
the same time your seat must push back as a counterbalance, the weight must be towards the balls of your
feet, and your knees will be slightly flexed and knocked
towards each other. Keeping your chin up off your chest
and eyes down will complete good posture, thereby
ensuring that your body turns out of the way to allow a
free arm swing (Fig 5.4). If you set up in this manner you
will be more likely to get your distance from the ball
correct. Many players who slice stand far too close to the
ball, which almost certainly guarantees an out-to-in swing
path (Fig 5.5).

Ball position

It is highly likely that you have been playing the ball too
near the left foot. This is a chicken and egg situation, but
any golfer who has open shoulders will have the ball too
near the left foot, and likewise anyone with the ball too
near the left foot will have open shoulders. So you must
now play the ball from a position nearer the centre of your
stance (Fig 5.6).

This will have a two-fold effect. First, it will help to
square up the shoulder line and consequently the swing
line; and secondly, when the ball is played too near the left
foot, the club head reaches the ball when it is starting to
move back inside the target line and is moving towards
the left of the target. Therefore it is likely that the ball will
start left of target.

I would suggest that for the meantime, you play all iron
shots with the back of the ball just forward of centre and
the driver about two inches inside the left heel.

You can check ball position either by placing one club
down across your toes and another behind the ball, or by
doing that and placing some tee pegs to mark your feet
position and then moving away and looking from the other
side. It is always easier to see the ball position from an
onlooker's viewpoint rather than from standing at the ball,
although personally I prefer to check my set up by looking

in a mirror. By playing the ball more centrally, you will find that the right shoulder does not want to stretch forward and out of line but will feel much lower than the left and further back than usual.

Weight distribution

The distribution of your weight at address can affect the swing significantly, and, in fact, weight distribution should change to match the shot you are playing.

With short irons, there is slightly more weight on the left side than the right.

With the rest of the irons and fairway woods, it is about even. When driving, there is slightly more weight on the right side than the left.

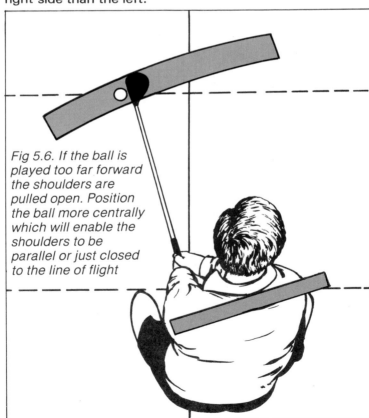

Fig 5.6. If the ball is played too far forward the shoulders are pulled open. Position the ball more centrally which will enable the shoulders to be parallel or just closed to the line of flight

The slicer tends to keep too much weight on the left foot at address for all shots, which restricts the shoulder turn and encourages a steep out-to-in swing. I would like you to set up with a 6 iron, and try to feel that your weight is even and towards the inside of each foot (Fig 5.3). Probably you have not been conscious of this before, and you can check it more easily by looking in the mirror.

Summary

The shape of the swing and the resultant shot are largely pre-determined at address. With a poor set up even the best golfers in the world will not hit the ball straight, so do not think that improving your set up is purely cosmetic — it is essential if you wish to improve.

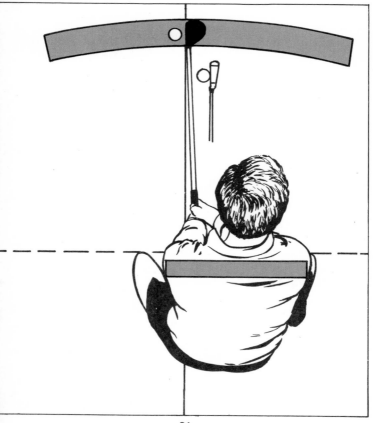

CHAPTER SIX

Correct hand action

Before you tackle the full swing, it is important that you have a clear understanding of the correct hand action. By now you should have a good grip, showing about two to two-and-a-half knuckles of the left hand and not gripping too tightly, and an improved set up. Therefore, you can now concentrate on just how the hands and arms should work in the impact area.

Swing the club back and stop when your hands reach hip height. At this point the back of your left hand should face forward and the toe of the club should be in the air, with the leading edge at right angles to the horizon (Fig 6.1). Due to the swinging weight of the club head, your wrists will be starting to cock upwards so that your left thumb is hinging towards the inside of your left forearm and the shaft is beyond the horizontal position. Provided that everything is correct here, then it should also be correct at the top. If the club face points towards the sky, then you have rolled your wrists and the club face open and you can regard this as being one of the major contributory factors to your slice (Fig 6.2).

Now swing the club head into the ball, allowing your forearms and hands to rotate slightly to the left and your wrists to uncock. This action will square the club face at impact, and you should find that by hip height on the through swing, the back of the right hand faces forward, and the toe of the club will again be in the air. As the right hand and arm rotate over the left after impact, the wrists will start to cock upwards and the left elbow will bend inwards and downwards, much as the right elbow does on the backswing. This will be an unfamiliar position to many of you since it is quite possible that your right hand has been working under rather than over your left through impact.

To emphasize the hand and arm action, put your feet together, which will help to keep out unwanted upper body action, and make this half-swing, quite gently at first, checking that everything is correct at hip height. Depending on how bad your hand action has been, you will feel that your hands, wrists and arms are much more active and freer, creating a slinging action of the club head into the ball. Club head speed will increase and, although

Fig 6.1. To develop good hand action, using a 6 iron with the ball teed low, swing back to hip height, where the back of the left hand should face forwards, toe of the club is in the air with the leading edge at right angles to the horizon. At hip height on the through swing the club should be in a similar position with the back of the right hand facing forwards. At the end of each half of the swing, the end of the grip should virtually point to the ball

at this stage the quality of strike may vary, the ball should start to fly with less curve on it. If this exercise is done correctly, you will find that the end of the grip points virtually at the ball at the completion of each half of the swing. Do not worry if at the end of the through swing the club face points slightly towards the ground — that is acceptable. What is unacceptable is a club face that points even slightly towards the sky (Fig 6.3). Once you have hit a few shots that fly straight, or with a slight right to left draw, you will have experienced correct hand and arm action through the impact zone, and the shot will feel sweeter off the clubface and will also fly further and lower than those that curve to the right.

This drill is best performed with the ball on a low tee, gripping down slightly on a 6 iron, which has just about

Fig 6.2. This shows a correct, square blade and an incorrect open blade position. In the correct position the back of the hand faces forward, not skyward

Fig 6.3. This is an incorrect position where the club face points towards the sky. Check this against Fig 6.1

the right amount of loft to allow sidespin to be more effective than backspin, and enabling you to get a true idea of how square the club head is at impact. The exercise serves to highlight hand action and hopefully starts to make your hands and arms less tense. It will also help you to swing the club on the correct plane and path. However, once your arms, body and legs start to play their part in the full swing, this hand action becomes somewhat diluted and less obvious as the swing gathers width. But without first being able to rid yourself of tension and the incorrect action, you would find it difficult to appreciate or incorporate the correct movements.

CHAPTER SEVEN

Starting correctly

By adopting the grip and set up described, you have every chance to start the backswing correctly, but I think it is important that you have a good picture in your mind's eye of what you are trying to do.

To correct any error in golf, it is usually necessary to feel that you are overdoing the correction, initially at least, and generally the change is not as big as it feels. As a slicer, your swing path has been very much from out-to-in, and in order to correct it you must try to swing from in-to-out. In clock face terms, you must convert from a 2 o'clock to 8 o'clock direction more towards the 4 o'clock to 10 o'clock line (Fig 2.1). As you address the ball it is essential that you can visualize where the club head should swing. When practising you can lightly score a mark in the grass in the 4 o'clock to 10 o'clock direction and try to swing along that line, or place some tee pegs in the ground just outside the correct line and try to swing just inside them.

Thus your pre-shot thoughts are important: if you can imagine where the club head should swing you have a better chance of making it happen.

The initial move

Most slicers do not turn the body sufficiently but make the backswing simply by swinging their arms and hands, so now you must feel that the left shoulder, left arm and shaft move away from the ball together (Fig 7.1). For most golfers, it is not natural to use the left arm, but by doing so you will engage the left shoulder muscles and start the turn correctly so that the triangle formed by the shoulders and arms at address moves away as one unit. The hands at this stage should feel passive and you must concentrate on turning your shoulders as the arms swing backwards and then up. You will notice that the club head will start back in a straight line and then turn inside much more than usual, and I would suggest that you lay another club down just outside the ball so that you can check this easily. The club head should move straight back without touching the club on the ground and then start to move

Fig 7.1. Feel that you start the backswing with the left arm and shoulder so that the triangle of the arms and shoulders remains intact. Starting in this manner will help keep the club head low to the ground

inside. The slightly closed eye line will also help you to envisage the correct path. Try to keep the club head lower to the ground than usual as this encourages the backswing to become a combined action between the shoulders and arms. Avoid any conscious hand or wrist action, especially excessive rotation to the right which will roll the clubface open. Since the shoulder and back muscles are large, they move slower than those in the hands and arms, so do not rush the backswing or you will not give the shoulders time to turn.

At the top

As the backswing continues, your body will be turning out of the way as your arms swing up, so that at the top of

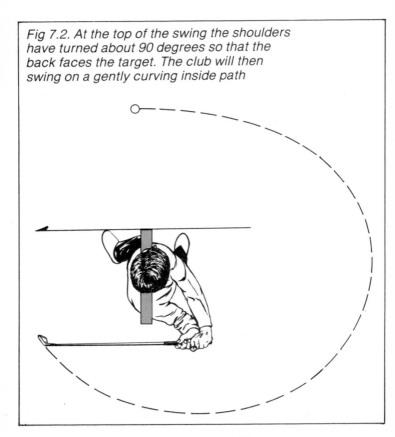

Fig 7.2. At the top of the swing the shoulders have turned about 90 degrees so that the back faces the target. The club will then swing on a gently curving inside path

the swing your back will be turned 90 degrees and your hips about 45 degrees (Fig 7.2). I have no doubt that you will feel a stretching sensation in your back muscles never before experienced. However, by closing the eye line it means that your head has rotated slightly to the right, which will make it easier to achieve a full turn. Check your swing in the mirror and you should find that the club shaft is virtually parallel to the line of flight (Fig 7.3) whereas many slicers have the shaft aimed left of target at this stage. This parallel position is vital if you are to be able to return to the ball from an inside path. Your weight should be mainly on the inside of your right leg, which should retain the flex it had at address and, depending on your flexibility, you may need to lift the left heel just off the ground. As the hips have turned, the left knee should now point just behind the ball.

The left arm should be slightly bowed, rather than perfectly straight or bent at the elbow, and the right arm should be folded with the elbow pointing to the ground. Main pressure will be felt in the last three fingers of the left hand which must not loosen on the grip. The left hand should have cocked so that the angle between the shaft and left arm is approximately 90 degrees. Provided that it has cocked correctly, i.e. flexed sideways rather than back on itself, the back of the left hand, arm and club face should be more or less in line. If your wrists have collapsed and there is excessive cupping at the back of the left wrist, you will probably find that the club face has turned open, i.e. the leading edge will be almost at right angles to the horizon (Fig 7.3 inset). This needs correcting. You may find that you have loosened the last three fingers of your left hand so keep them firm. If this is not the answer, then you may have turned your wrists open too much, possibly just as the club moved away from the ball. If this applies to you, then you must make certain that you initiate the backswing with the left shoulder, left arm and shaft moving away together, keeping your hands passive. Check the club position halfway back, making sure that the blade is at right angles to the horizon. Alternatively, you may just need to control the clubhead better at the top of the swing. When the shoulders fail to turn, there is a great deal of pressure on the wrists at the top of the swing, and inevitably they tend to collapse under this pressure. Now by turning your shoulders more fully, you are spreading the load of the swing and should control the club head better at the top.

As a reasonable guide, the arms should swing into the gap between your right shoulder and head, and for those of you who have been lacking a decent shoulder turn, your hands will feel lower and further behind you than usual. This is because the shoulders have provided an unaccustomed turning element to the swing, consequently altering its entire feel. The plane, i.e. the angle of incline of the swing, is flattened, making your attack on the ball shallower and providing more forward and less downward force to result in more powerful shots.

However, the 'wrist rollers' among you may feel that your arms have swung higher than usual, and this is correct. Excessive clockwise hand and arm rotation in the backswing flattens the swing and thus when you eliminate the roll, the plane becomes slightly more upright which is correct. Your action now should feel that you swing your arms much more up and down in the swing, thus preventing you from casting the club to the outside. You should check this new position in a mirror so that you can see how good it looks — just like a professional!

There are two good exercises that will help you to improve your backswing. Place a club behind your back and under your arms and then, bending slightly forward as in the good address position, turn to your right and left. This will help to stretch your back muscles and put you into the correct position at the top of the backswing.

Find a sidehill slope, where the ball would be positioned above your feet and practise swinging there. This will make your shoulders turn more readily and flatten your arm swing, causing you then to swing from in-to-in. Or alternatively, imagine that the ball is teed at shoulder

height so that you hold the club horizontally in front of you. From this position, swing the club making sure that your shoulders turn to the right and then to the left as your arms swing. By gradually lowering the height of the imaginary tee and repeating the swing, you will start to appreciate and experience how the shoulders must turn in the swing.

Although golf is not a series of positions, but a continuous swing, it is necessary when altering your game to be able to isolate and feel new positions. You will be able to groove your backswing by being aware of the correct new position at the top. By checking it in a mirror you will also get a visual input which will serve as an additional reminder as well as helping you to see that everything looks as it should.

Fig 7.3. Ideally the shaft at the top of the swing is parallel to the target, the club face is still square and in line with the back of the forearm with the right elbow pointing to the ground. In the inset drawing, due to the wrists collapsing the club face has been turned open so that the leading edge is almost at right angles to the horizon

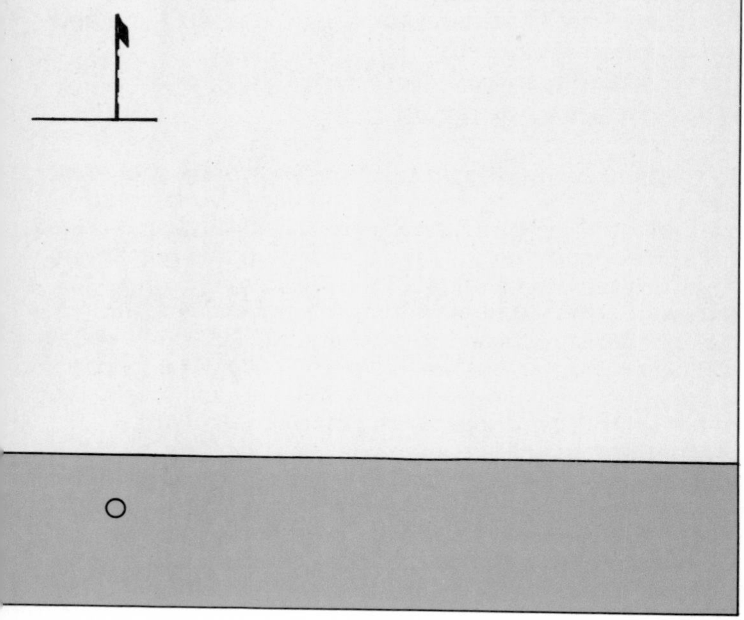

CHAPTER EIGHT

The change of direction

The change of direction from backswing to downswing is perhaps the most crucial part in the swing as even with a perfect backswing, things can still go wrong at this point. For most beginners, it is hard to appreciate that the hands and arms are going to provide most of the power when in fact they feel so weak. What you must realise is that it is club head speed that is of the essence, and hands and arms can move much quicker than the body. However, clubhead speed is only of consequence if the face is square and travelling from the correct angle and in the direction of the target at impact — all factors that you are working towards.

Remember, however, that you are trying to *swing* the club head back to the ball and *not* heave your body towards the target. Unfortunately for the beginner and higher handicap player, it is the right shoulder area at the top of the swing that feels most powerful, and so often the downswing is initiated by throwing the right shoulder forwards towards the ball (Fig 8.1). This only serves to set the swing onto a steep out-to-in path, and the hand and arm action gets blocked.

The correct way down

On the backswing, the right side of your body should be turned out of the way to create a space in which your arms should swing backwards and upwards, and it is into this same space that they must swing on the way down. You must feel that instead of moving the right shoulder first, your arms should swing *down* into this gap and your back should stay turned to the target (Fig 8.2). To you it will feel as though you are liable to hit the ball a long way to the right, which indeed might well happen initially, but do not worry about that for the moment. Instead, concentrate on pulling down with your *left* arm, without your shoulders turning back. This, of course, will not be what is happening, but remember that until now your shoulders have been far too active at this point, and so you must feel that the start of the downswing has no shoulder motion at all. In clock face terms, you will now

Fig 8.1. At the top of the swing it is the right shoulder area that feels most powerful and is usually thrown forward casting the club onto an outside path

be able to swing the club down more from the 4 o'clock, rather than 2 o'clock, direction.

Downswing faults

Many problems with the change of direction come about because the player is so keen to hit the ball *forward,* and this translates into a forward movement with the right side creating an outside approach to the ball. If instead you can think of the downswing as being a *downward* movement of your arms, then you are more likely to keep the club head on an inside path. The right shoulder will then turn much more under the left, rather than forward and across it. The forward element of the swing will come about naturally as your body eventually turns through the shot.

Another cause of throwing the club head onto an outside path is rushing from the top, which tends to allow the right side to overpower the left. Instead, the change of direction should be smooth and unhurried so that the left arm can keep control. As your arms swing down you must feel that your left knee moves towards the target, which will start to transfer your weight onto the left side. However, this must not be a jerky or violent action but should be a smooth movement, complementing the arm swing. It is easy to overdo leg action, which can spin the left side out of the way too much, and pull the right side forward creating the out-to-in swing that you are trying to cure. So feel that the left knee moves laterally towards the target at the same time as the left arm pulls down. You can practise the correct change of direction movements without the ball, perhaps with the mirror to your right, so that you can check that the club stays on that inside path.

The head position can also help or hinder at this stage. Prior to the backswing, you set the eye line closed by rotating the head slightly to the right; at the start of the downswing, try to maintain that same position, so that you are looking at the ball mainly with your left eye and your head does not move towards the target either laterally or in a rotary motion. This will help to keep you on that inside track, but once you approach the impact zone it is quite in order for it to be rotating fractionally to the left.

Fig 8.2. At the start of the downswing the arms should swing down into the space created by the right side moving out of the way on the backswing. It may help you to keep the club on the inside by feeling that your back stays turned to the target as your arms swing down. The left knee should move laterally towards your target which will encourage an inside attack

CHAPTER NINE

Impact and beyond

Having started the downswing on the correct track, i.e. from the inside, you must now allow your hands and arms to work through the impact zone much as described earlier in Chapter 6. So as the club head approaches impact, both hands and arms will be rotating to the left and your wrists will be straightening, squaring the club face. To the better golfer, who has trained his or her hands to work correctly in the swing, this becomes very much a matter of free-wheeling through impact to the finish, allowing the centrifugal force of the swing to assist in the squaring of the club face. But to the golfer who has been gripping the club too tightly and has not experienced a decent club head release too often, it will mean consciously having to work on squaring the club face. At this stage it is important also to remember the swing path

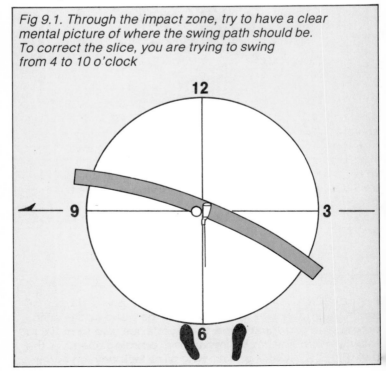

Fig 9.1. Through the impact zone, try to have a clear mental picture of where the swing path should be. To correct the slice, you are trying to swing from 4 to 10 o'clock

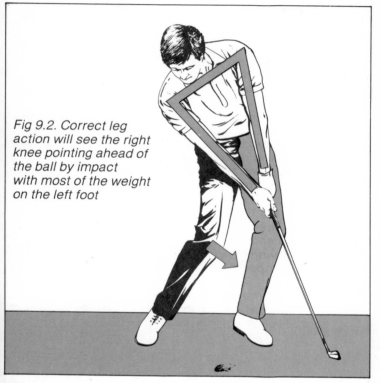

Fig 9.2. Correct leg action will see the right knee pointing ahead of the ball by impact with most of the weight on the left foot

direction, i.e. 4 o'clock to 10 o'clock (Fig 9.1) and feel that as your arms are swung down towards the ball, they are not only rotating to the left but also swinging away from your body towards the right of the target. This is the way that someone who draws the ball plays, and it is a good antidote to the slice. As the arms swing past the ball the body must continue turning so that both at impact, and just beyond, the triangular relationship between the arms and shoulders is intact.

Leg action

I wrote that at the start of the downswing you should move your left knee towards the target, and as the swing progresses you must allow the right knee also to move in this direction so that by impact it is pointing ahead of the ball (Fig 9.2). Many golfers who slice lack any leg action,

47

and if you are someone who has most of their weight on the right foot at impact (Fig 9.3) then you must emphasize the leg action somewhat so that you finish with most of your weight on the outside left foot with the right heel off the ground and the right toes providing the balance. It is helpful to move your right knee towards your left at impact in order to get to this position. You must also allow your head to rotate towards the target once you have hit the ball so that you finish looking forward with your body in the same direction. Most of my pupils create good leg action by trying to swing to this balanced finish position, because if you can get to that position, then your legs must have worked well (Fig 9.4). Timing them to move at exactly the right moment comes with practice, but once you realise what the legs should be doing, at least you have a sporting chance of attaining the correct action.

Fig 9.3. The golfer who does not use his legs correctly leaves too much weight on the right leg on the downswing and through impact

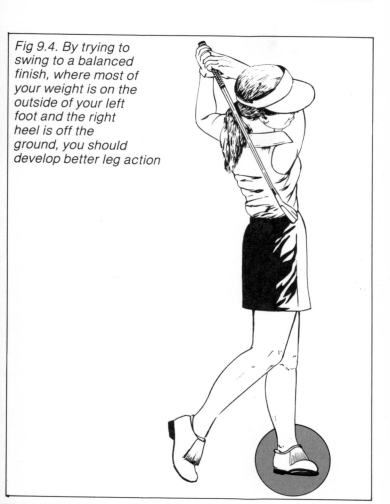

Fig 9.4. By trying to swing to a balanced finish, where most of your weight is on the outside of your left foot and the right heel is off the ground, you should develop better leg action

Left side strengthening

Most people who play golf right-handed are right-handed, which usually means that their left side is quite weak. It is therefore beneficial to strengthen the left side, as it plays an important guiding role in the swing. Grip a 6 iron with the left hand only and place the right hand over the left instead of on the grip. Without a ball, make your backswing and you will naturally be using your left side, just as you should in the two-handed swing. As you swing down you will feel your left arm pulling, rather than the

right side throwing the club. Complete the swing, but at
impact take your right hand off the club. You will
automatically swing through the ball, rather than stop at
it, and finish facing your target with your weight on your
left side and the right heel off the ground. This exercise
not only promotes left side control but also encourages
the body and legs to work correctly beyond impact. If at
the beginning, the club feels too heavy, grip down it
slightly. Gradually build up the number of swings, but take
care not to over-exercise at first — perhaps 10 to 15
swings twice a day would be sufficient, depending on
your strength.

Action and reaction

At first it will be hard for you to accept that in order to
stop the ball going to the right, you need to have the
feeling of hitting in that direction. Earlier in this book, I
explained in some detail how the slicer is born, i.e. lack of
correct hand action leaves the club face open — spinning
the ball to the right so that the golfer starts to hit across to
the left. But if you work on developing your hand and arm
action to square the blade at impact, the ball will no longer
curve to the right and this will encourage you to start to
attack the ball from the correct inside path. I have
suggested that you envisage this as being in the 4 o'clock
to 10 o'clock direction, but some people may even have to
exaggerate that example so that at first you *feel* as though
you are swinging from 5 o'clock in order to correct your
extreme out-to-in swing. Eventually, as your hand and
arm action improves, you will have more confidence to
commit yourself to that feeling of swinging to the right of
the target and will ultimately be able to start the ball just
right of the target and draw it back.

If you find that it starts consistently too much to the
right, you will know then that a lot of your hard work is
over and that you can now swing the club head back to
the ball from the inside. You may need to move the ball a
little nearer the left foot and square up your shoulders at
address so that your swing path will be more in the 3.30 to
9 o'clock direction.

As your hand action improves you may have to weaken
the grip if you find that the ball is now curving too much
to the left. This is fine tuning and very much a personal
thing.

CHAPTER TEN

The pull

The pull is the shot that starts left and continues in that direction with no curve to the flight (Fig 2.4a). I am dealing with this shot now since it belongs to the same family as the slice, i.e. the out-to-in swing path, and, generally speaking, someone who slices will also pull some shots. Remember that the straighter faced clubs will impart more sidespin than the lofted clubs, and so if you slice with your 4 iron you may well pull your 9 iron, since the strong backspin from the shot over-rides the sidespin and the ball flies straight left (Fig 10.1). If your shots fall into this category, then really you should consider yourself

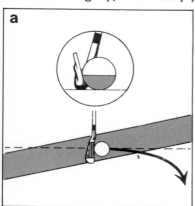

a

Fig 10.1a. When using a straighter faced club, swinging on an out-to-in swing path with an open club face, the ball will start left then fade to the right. Because the ball is hit nearer its equator, more sidespin is imparted which eventually curves the ball to the right

Fig 10.1b. The same swing with a more lofted club will pull the ball straight left of the target because the more lofted club strikes the ball low down, imparting strong backspin which over-rides the sidespin

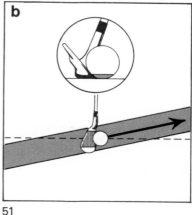

b

a slicer rather than someone who pulls shots.

However, if you tend to pull all of your shots, then it would seem that your hand action, and consequently club face alignment, is fine but the direction of the swing path is incorrect. First you muct check your set up, using the methods described in Chapter 5. You may discover that you have been aiming straight left instead of at the target. Therefore you should practise with the two clubs on the ground until the new line up becomes familiar. In this new set up you will be more aware of seeing your left shoulder in your vision when you look towards the target.

You might have been aiming left because the ball was too far forward in your stance, which has the effect of pulling the shoulders open at address and thereby setting

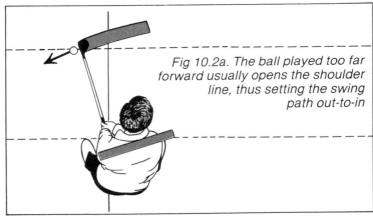

Fig 10.2a. The ball played too far forward usually opens the shoulder line, thus setting the swing path out-to-in

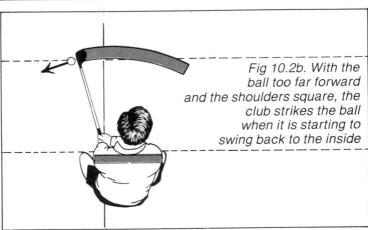

Fig 10.2b. With the ball too far forward and the shoulders square, the club strikes the ball when it is starting to swing back to the inside

the swing path out-to-in in relation to the target
(Fig 10.2a). Place the ball more centrally in your stance
and check that your shoulder line is parallel to the target.

If your shoulders are square but the ball is still too far
forward, you will hit it when the club head starts to move
back to the inside rather than when it is travelling directly
towards the target (Fig 10.2b). Adjust the ball position
until your shots start on target.

Alternatively, you could be aiming too far right, and
then coming over the top of the ball (Fig 10.2c). Just like
the golfer who slices, you can either be aiming too far left
or right and create a pulled shot.

Whichever set up error you make, it will be helpful if
you have clubs on the ground in order to convince you
that the adjustments are correct. If your set up and ball
position seem satisfactory but your shots still go left, it
must be because you are still swinging from out-to-in. If
this is the case, you should re-read Chapters 7, 8 and 9
and work to improve both the takeaway and downswing,
making sure that you have a strong mental picture of
where the club head must swing on that corrective 4 to 10
o'clock path. Do not make the backswing just by lifting
your arms up; be certain that you also have a good
shoulder which will help to keep the club on an inside
path. Do not rush the change of direction for the
downswing, but concentrate on swinging your arms
down, feeling that the club is swung to the right of the
target. Hitting shots that *feel* half- to three-quarters power
will help to keep the club on that correct inside track.

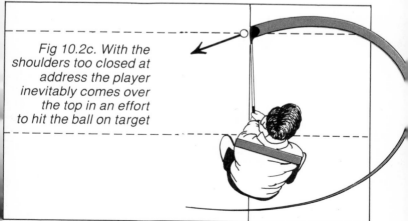

Fig 10.2c. With the shoulders too closed at address the player inevitably comes over the top in an effort to hit the ball on target

CHAPTER ELEVEN

The pull hook

It is important to differentiate between the beginner who hits the occasional pull hook and the golfer who hits it more regularly. As a beginner, if you swing from out-to-in and are inconsistent with club face alignment at impact, you will inevitably hit a few shots that start left and then curve left (Fig 2.4c). In this instance, the club face was closed, i.e. facing left of the swing path at impact. For the beginner the shot will usually go quite low and not very far, and is a symptom of the fact that until you have played and practised a little longer you will continue to hit a variety of shots. The main cures have already been detailed and you must go back to checking the basics, such as grip, set up and ball position. You must try to swing along the 4 to 10 o'clock swing path line and make certain that you keep your hands and arms swinging through the ball — not just at it. If the body stops turning or the arms slow down, the hands carry on and close the club face too quickly (Fig 11.1). So instead of thinking about hitting at the ball, look upon the swing as making a big circle with the club head, and striking the ball within that circle.

The consistent pull hook

However, if you consistently hit shots that go quite a long way but always start left and turn left at the end of their flight, apply the same corrections as for the pull (see Chapter 10) to correct your swing path. You should also check that your grip is not too strong, i.e. hands turned too far to the right, and experiment with a weaker grip. It is quite acceptable to draw the ball under control, i.e. where the ball curves only a few yards in flight, as this is, in fact, a powerful shot, but if the club face becomes too closed at impact a hooking flight is the result, which is usually very destructive. You may also need to smarten up your foot and leg action, ensuring that as you swing your arms down, your weight is transferred from your right foot back to the left (Fig 9.2) and that your hips continue turning towards the target so that your hands and arms

Fig 11.1. If the body stops turning and arms stop swinging through the shot, the hands will quickly turn the club face closed resulting in a shot that curves from right to left

have room to square the club face gradually (Fig 17.1). You should also practise the following half swing drill, which will emphasize quieter hands in balance with the correct body turn and arm swing.

Half swing exercise

Using a 6 iron, grip down the handle and take a wider stance than normal for the club. Practise a half swing in which the triangle of the shoulders and arms at address turns to the right, then swings through impact and remains intact until hip height on the follow through (Fig 11.2). Feel that you are trying to swing the club more by the effort of your body turn and arm swing (which the set up should encourage) than by active hand action. You are trying to educate your hands and arms rather than just swish them about aimlessly in the swing. The swing should feel wider than your normal action both on the backswing and through swing. Hit about 20 shots like this and then make your usual swing. You should feel that your hands are working more within the body turn and arm swing rather than indpendently. The more erratic beginner should practise this exercise as well as the one outlined in Chapter 6 in order to ingrain the right balance of hand, arm and body action.

However, one word of warning about this exercise: whereas the wider stance encourages firmer wrists, it tends also to restrict leg action, so make sure that you do not swing flat-footed! To further promote awareness of swinging *through* the ball, practise the left side strengthening drill (detailed near the end of Chapter 9).

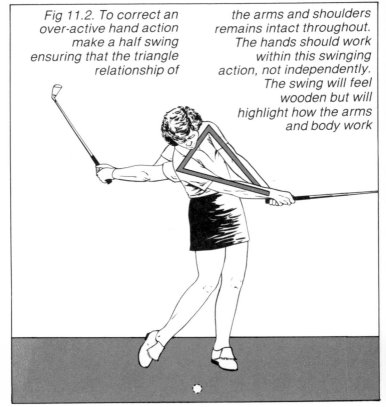

Fig 11.2. To correct an over-active hand action make a half swing ensuring that the triangle relationship of the arms and shoulders remains intact throughout. The hands should work within this swinging action, not independently. The swing will feel wooden but will highlight how the arms and body work

CHAPTER TWELVE

The straight slice

We have now covered all shots possible from an out-to-in swing path, and before tackling the in-to-out family of shots, I want to deal with those players whose swing path is correct, i.e. in-to-in, but whose shots start towards the target and then veer to the right. This is because the clubface is open at impact.

If your shots are in this category you should check first that your grip is not too weak, i.e. your hands are not turned too much to the left on the grip (Fig 12.1). If this is the case, you should move them until you can see two to two-and-a-half knuckles of the left hand, which should have the effect of squaring the club face (Figs 4.1-4.4).

Also check that you are addressing the ball with the club face square to the target; it is easy to fall into bad habits in this respect and not to realise that the face is out of line.

If your grip and club face alignment seem okay, make certain that your hand action is correct and lively enough, since you may be opening the clubface on the backswing with excessive hand and arm rotation and/or blocking the

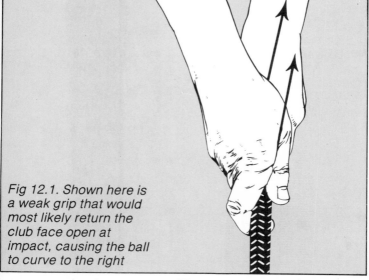

Fig 12.1. Shown here is a weak grip that would most likely return the club face open at impact, causing the ball to curve to the right

action through impact. Practise as described in Chapter 6 until the shots go straight, allowing the right hand and arm to rotate over the left just after impact. If your grip is good and you feel that you are rotating your hands and arms correctly, you could be doing one of two things: either not transferring your weight sufficiently on the backswing (Fig 12.2) and/or moving too much towards the target on the downswing. On the backswing, the weight must transfer to the right side so that about 80 per cent rests on the right leg at the top of the swing. As the downswing starts, the weight moves back to the left so that all momentum is in the direction of the target. The left hip and the body continue turning out of the way, giving your arms a clear passage to swing through and square the club face. If you fail to transfer your weight to the right on the backswing — often brought about by trying to keep the head still — it will move onto the left leg and will then transfer back to the right during the downswing. Consequently the left side does not clear out of the way and the hands and arms cannot fully release to square the club face. If you are in this category, the correction will

Fig 12.2. If the correct weight transference is not made in the backswing, too much weight remains on the left foot, often brought about by trying to keep the head absolutely still

make you *feel* that you are swaying to the right in the backswing as you turn the right side out of the way. Do not worry about keeping your head absolutely still but keep it steady with your eyes on the ball, and make certain that you feel the weight going onto the right leg, which must retain its original flex. Having turned on the backswing you will now be able to transfer your weight back to the left side and then continue turning the left side out of the way as the arms swing through. Feel that the right knee moves towards the left at impact, which helps to turn the left side smoothly out of the way.

If you feel that you make a good weight transference but still slice the ball, it might be that you are getting ahead of the ball at impact (Fig 12.3) and in that position the hands are unable to release. You will have to feel that from the top of the swing, you look at the back of the ball very carefully and try to stay behind the shot. You may need to put more emphasis on an arm swing and less on your leg action. There are plenty of photographs of top professionals who use a strong leg action at the start of the downswing. They match this with a very strong hand and arm action that few club golfers possess. Do not be lulled into copying this strong leg action when all it will do is prevent your hands and arms delivering the club head squarely into the back of the ball at impact. Practising hitting balls with your feet together will make you appreciate the role of your hands and arms.

Fig 12.3. If you move too much ahead of the ball, you will not be able to release the club head at impact and it will remain open

CHAPTER THIRTEEN

The in-to-out swing

If you consistently manage to swing the club head along an in-to-out path then you should not be too far away from becoming a reasonably good golfer. You may find it hard to believe if you fall into this category since you may also be capable of hitting the most horrendously destructive shots as well, and so may quite possibly possess a high handicap. As you will realise by now, the ideal swing path is from in-to-in, and for the beginner, the hardest part in golf is to bring the club head back to the ball from an inside path. You can already do this but cannot yet hit the ball while the club head is travelling towards the target since your club is still travelling towards the outside, i.e. right of the target, at impact. Having conquered the hardest part, you will be pleased to learn that your corrections are far easier to master than for the inveterate slicer. It will be helpful to review the sort of shots that are likely from an in-to-out swing path:

▶ When the clubface is square at impact, the ball will go straight right (Fig 2.5a).
▶ When the clubface is open the ball will start right and then turn to the right (Fig 2.5b).
▶ When the clubface is closed, the ball will start right and then turn to the left (Fig 2.5c).

The player who has a well developed hand action has no problem in squaring the clubface at impact, and indeed very often closes it. He/she is therefore more than likely to start to swing from the inside, knowing that the ball will turn to the left in flight. Under control, this type of shot, the draw, is one of the most powerful, and indeed most satisfying, of golf shots, which I am sure would satisfy all golfers. However, when the draw becomes too strong, it turns into a hook with which no golfer would be happy.

Players who swing from in-to-out are often those who underwent a course of golf lessons and consequently understand the need for an inside attack and good hand action. Therefore, rather than suggest they have bad habits they have simply exaggerated the good ones. They generally hit the ball a fair distance but might experience trouble with shots from bare lies. They may also be better hitting a 3 wood than a driver, since closing the clubface on a driver can produce an unpleasant duck (quick) hook quite easily. If the club face becomes excessively shut at impact, the ball will hook low and left very quickly, despite the player swinging to the right of the target. In this instance, the very shut club face has over-ridden the swing path and sent the ball immediately left.

The in-to-out swing tends to be on the flat side often causing the club head to swing through the impact zone on a sharply curving path. As the club head curves sharply, it is not travelling directly towards the target for very long before it swings back to the inside (Fig 13.1). It is therefore quite common for someone with a flat swing to be able to hit shots a long way right or a long way left, depending on the part of the arc in which contact is made with the ball.

We will analyse the factors that can cause a hook in the same way in which we dealt with the slice, i.e. getting the basics right first.

Fig 13.1. The player who hooks tends to swing the club head on a flat, sharply curving arc so that it does not travel directly toward the target for very long. It is therefore easy to hit shots that go right and left of target

CHAPTER FOURTEEN

The strong grip

The purpose of the grip is to return the club face to the ball in a square position without any undue or independent manipulation. The player who flights the ball from right to left has his/her hands on the grip in such a way that the club face is closed at impact (Fig 14.1), and the more closed it is, the stronger the curve in flight.

I would recommend that you re-read Chapter 4 in which I described the most important aspects of the grip. However, in your case, you should grip with only two knuckles of the left hand showing and the 'V's pointing more towards the chin and right ear (Fig 14.2). The right hand, especially the triggered forefinger, must sit much

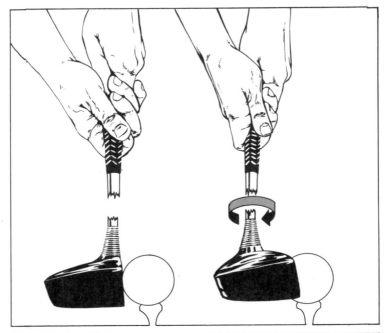

Fig 14.1. When the hands are turned too much to the right on the grip, they return to a more neutral position at impact thus closing the club face

more to the side of the grip than underneath it, with the club resting more at the base of the fingers than in the palm of the hand. Make certain that the left thumb sits snugly into the hollow of the right hand as this will help to make the two hands work as a unit. With your hands in this position, the palm of the right and back of the left will be facing towards the target. If by any chance you grip with two hands completely on the club, I would suggest that you try the overlapping grip, where the little finger of the right hand sit on top of the left forefinger. This change will again make your hands act as more of a unit and put a little more authority in the left hand. You may also find that a *slightly* firmer grip will help to stabilize your hand action, which previously may have been working too independently of the rest of your swing.

The player with a very strong grip who has virtually four knuckles on the left hand showing might read the above explanation of the grip and wonder how it is that he/she still hits the ball with left to right curve on it. This player has turned the hands so far to the right that at impact the heel, instead of the back, of the left hand is facing the target. By rotating the forearms and hands correctly, he/she would be lucky to get the ball off the ground, as the club face would be so closed. His/her grip allows and indeed encourages swinging the club to the inside on the backswing, but then blocks his/her action through impact. It may sound strange but to square the club face this player must weaken his/her grip. I will outline the swing corrections in Chapter 18.

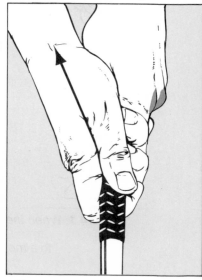

Fig 14.2. The player whose shots curve too much from right to left should grip the club so that he can see about 2 knuckles of his left hand. The 'V's point between the chin and right ear and the right forefinger sits at the side of the shaft, not underneath it

CHAPTER FIFTEEN

The closed set up

The golfer who closes the club face at impact, curving the ball to the left, will soon start to aim to the right to allow for the curve (Fig 15.1). But much like the slicer who believes that aiming left is the cure when in fact it compounds the error, so the golfer who hooks, makes matters worse by aiming to the right. Not only will the club face be shut at impact but the club head will approach so much from inside the target line that additional hook spin will be imparted on the ball. It becomes a vicious circle (and a vicious hook for that matter) and one that is first broken by checking the grip and then the set up.

Since you tend to swing along the line of your body, ideally you should try to stand parallel to the intended line of flight so that you may swing correctly from in-to-in, i.e. the club head approaches the ball from between 3 and 4 o'clock and strikes the ball whilst swinging towards 9 o'clock. In the closed stance, a line across the shoulders would point considerably right of the target, more in the

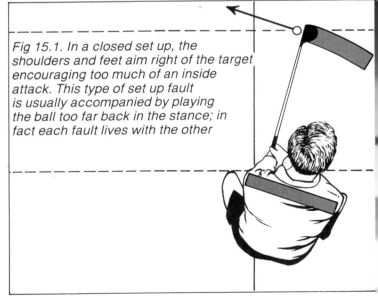

Fig 15.1. In a closed set up, the shoulders and feet aim right of the target encouraging too much of an inside attack. This type of set up fault is usually accompanied by playing the ball too far back in the stance; in fact each fault lives with the other

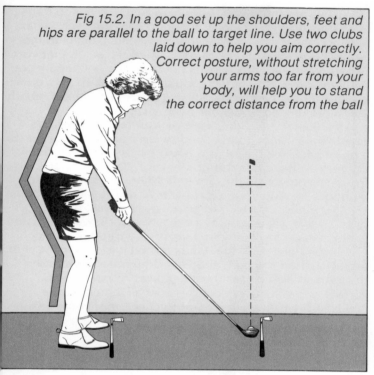

Fig 15.2. In a good set up the shoulders, feet and hips are parallel to the ball to target line. Use two clubs laid down to help you aim correctly. Correct posture, without stretching your arms too far from your body, will help you to stand the correct distance from the ball

direction of 4 to 10 o'clock, which will then tend to set the swing from in-to-out.

Checking the address position

With a target to aim at, address the ball and then place a club down across the line of your toes. You will be able to see if your stance is closed. But also check your shoulder line, either by holding a club across the shoulders yourself or by getting a friend to do this and telling you exactly where the shaft points. Remember that it should be parallel to the target. You can also check this in a mirror, standing with the mirror to your right, and if they are closed, you will be able to see quite a lot of your left shoulder and a club across the shoulders will point to the right.

To help correct your set up, place two clubs on the ground, one just outside the ball and the other about

18 inches nearer to you, both parallel to the ball to target line. Now address the ball, trying to get your feet, knees, hips and most importantly your shoulders parallel to the clubs. Look towards the target several times, so that you become familiar with how it should appear, no longer are you looking over your left shoulder at it (Fig 15.2). You will also find it helpful to use an intermediate target, about 2 to 3 feet ahead of the ball over which to aim.

An adjustment of the angle of your feet may also be worthwhile. Most golfers who swing from in-to-out, make a good backswing turn, but often fail to clear their body, i.e. turn sufficiently through the shot. You might benefit from placing your right foot at right angles to the line of flight but angling your left foot towards the target at about 15-20°. It may also help to have your feet just a touch open as this will restrict any excessive backswing turn and make it easier to clear your hips on the through swing.

A strong grip with the hands turned well under the club tends to make the right shoulder drop much lower than the left and also closes the shoulders. Hopefully your correct grip will now make shoulder alignment easier.

It is also worthwhile for you to check that your eye line

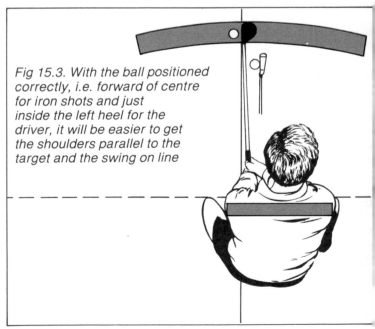

Fig 15.3. With the ball positioned correctly, i.e. forward of centre for iron shots and just inside the left heel for the driver, it will be easier to get the shoulders parallel to the target and the swing on line

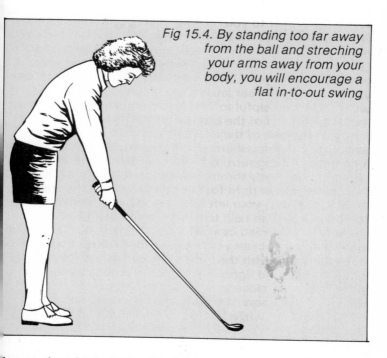

Fig 15.4. By standing too far away from the ball and streching your arms away from your body, you will encourage a flat in-to-out swing

is not aimed too far to the right, giving you a distorted view of the correct target line.

In correcting the set up for the slice, I recommend that it would be helpful for the player to practise the address position standing either on square patio slabs or kitchen floor tiles, or by using two clubs laid down parallel to the target. The same holds true for the player who sets up closed, as these guide lines will help to convince you that you are now lined up correctly. They will also prove useful in checking that the club face is square at address.

Ball position

A closed set up is often accompanied by playing the ball too far back in the stance, which in itself will encourage the shoulders to close (Fig 15.1). Check that the ball for your iron shots is played forward of centre in your stance, which will help to square the shoulders (Fig 15.3). Play the ball for the driver only just inside the left heel. It is difficult to be exact about ball position because so much depends on the width of stance, but experiment with playing it in a more forward position for all shots. With the ball back you may have found that your hands were a long way ahead of the ball at address so that there was a forward angle between your left arm and the shaft. This situation tends to make the club head swing too much to the inside at the start of the backswing. Therefore when you re-position the ball, check that your hands for the irons are only just ahead of the ball with the left arm and shaft forming a straighter line than before. With the driver, I would recommend that the straight line still exists with the back of the left hand approximately level with the front of the ball. Apart from the ball being too far back in the stance causing a closed shoulder line, you are also more likely to strike the ball whilst the club head is still swinging from the inside and so the ball starts out to the right. By moving it forwards, you have a better chance of making contact while the club is swinging directly towards the target.

Distance from the ball

The golfer who hooks will often be standing too far away from the ball at address (Fig 15.4) which will encourage a flat, in-to-out swing. To correct this, stand erect with the club held out horizontally in front of you with your hands at waist height. Now lower it to the ground by bending from the hip bones. Do not stretch your arms too far away from your body — the upper part of the arms should be quite close to your body. If you bend sufficiently from the hips, the arms will just hang more or less in the space created. Now flex your knees slightly and you should be in a good address position, having the correct posture and distance from the ball (Fig 15.2).

CHAPTER SIXTEEN

The swing

In your corrected address position, it is important for you to be aware of the new direction of the target. Until now you have looked at it over your left shoulder, which is no longer the case. Take two or three glances towards the target and then try to see the direction in which the club head must approach the ball. This will help to give you a better picture of the overall swing, and consequently you will be better equipped to start the backswing on the right track.

Swing path

In clock face terms, you need to see that the swing path is more in the direction of 3.30 to 9 o'clock rather than 4 to 10 o'clock (Fig 16.1). To this end, it will probably help if you can start the club head back towards 3 o'clock for a longer period of time than before, and feel that your arms

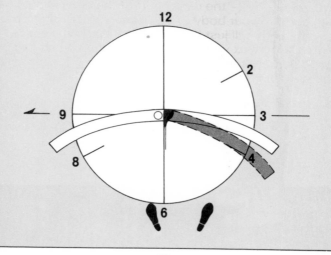

Fig 16.1. From the improved set up you need to visualize the correct backswing path. Ideally for the golfer who has swung too much on the inside, he should imagine it as 3.30 to 9 o'clock

swing more up and down rather than behind you. Most golfers who swing too much from the inside have a good enough shoulder turn, so concentrate a little more on what your arms are doing.

The top of the swing

At the top of the swing, your back should be turned to the target and your arms should be positioned in the gap between your right shoulder and your head. If you have had a flat arm swing, your hands will now feel more above your head than your right shoulder (Fig 16.2). Again, this is only a relative feeling and ideally they will be in the correct slot. If you can practise on a sidehill lie with the

Fig 16.2. At the top you will find your hands and arms are higher than before, more above your head than behind it, with the club face square to the plane

Fig 16.3. Excessive cupping of the left wrist will raise the right elbow and cause the shaft to aim well right of the target with the club face open

ball below your feet, this will make you swing your arms more upright in the backswing and put less emphasis on your body turning too much. The club should also be about parallel to the target line, but golfers who hook often find that it points to the right at the top of the swing. Hopefully the improved set up and backswing path will have gone a long way to curing this problem, but if the shaft still points excessively to the right, check that for the first twelve inches of the takeaway the club swings away on a *gently* curving inside path. If that seems satisfactory but the shaft is still well across the line, you might be collapsing your wrists at the top so make certain that there is not excessive cupping at the back of your left wrist (Fig 16.3). It should be almost in line with the left forearm. If you are very supple, you may just be swinging rather a long way which inevitably means that the shaft must cross the line. This is acceptable provided that you can turn back in a co-ordinated fashion. However, you would probably benefit by putting more emphasis on your arms swinging rather than the body turning, and by making what feels to you to be a three-quarter length backswing from which you will find it easier to swing the club more towards the target through impact. This will emphasize your through swing rather than your backswing and make the swing feel more controlled.

Club face alignment

You should also ensure that the club face is square, i.e.
positioned between facing the sky and facing forwards,
and approximately in line with the back of the left hand
and forearm. If it points to the sky, i.e. closed, check that
your grip is still not too strong. If you have arched the
back of your left wrist, then this will close the club face
and you should adjust this position until the left thumb is
under the shaft at this stage. Check that at hip height the
club face is at right angles to the horizon and not pointing
towards the ground.

However, it is also possible to hook the ball from an
open club face position at the top of the swing. The
hands, having turned the club face open by working too
independently on the backswing, respond in a similar
manner on the downswing and turn the club face closed
prior to impact. You must try to make the initial part of the
backswing more co-ordinated with the triangle of the arms
and shoulders moving away together, and allow the wrists
to cock purely in response to the swinging weight of the
club head. Do not roll the hands but ensure that the left
thumb moves sideways towards the inside of the left
forearm.

The downswing

With your hands hopefully now in a higher position at the
top of the backswing, you will inevitably be able to swing
back to the ball on a better path, not so much from the
inside but more straight on towards the target. Therefore,
at the start of the downswing, you should feel that the left
arm is in command and pulls down at the same time as
the left knee moves laterally towards the target (Fig 8.2).
You may be someone who flattens the plane of their
swing too much on the downswing, by dropping the right
elbow in towards the right hip. This action, if not
overdone, is commendable but since you swing too much
from in-to-out, guard against jamming the right elbow into
your side at this stage. Instead you should feel that you
are pulling the end of the grip directly towards the ball so
that the club will approach from a steeper but more
correct plane than before and not so much from the
inside.

Since you hook, or over-draw the ball, it is possible that your leg action has not been sufficiently lively, which has allowed your hands and arms to become too active through impact, thus closing the club face. In the downswing you should feel your weight move onto your left side as your arms swing down, but do make sure that your head remains steady throughout.

Impact and beyond

In the impact area you must feel that as your *arms* are swinging *through* the ball, you allow your body to turn through as well, preserving the triangular relationship (Fig 9.2). So often a player who hooks the ball, stops his/her arms swinging and the body from turning. Consequently the right hand closes quickly over the left, shutting the club face (Fig 11.1). Players who swing too much from in-to-out usually have well developed hand action, but in order to be effective this action must work on swinging arms, so always be sure to keep the left arm moving through the swing.

The right side of the body turns out of the way in the backswing and the left side must react similarly in the downswing (Fig 17.1), thus creating a space in which the arms can swing and enabling the club face to remain square to the target for just a split second longer rather than becoming closed too quickly. Provided that you have a neutral grip, as already described, at impact you should feel that the back of the left hand is facing the target for a longer period of time. You should also sense that the club head is swinging down the target line, i.e. towards 9 o'clock, rather than to the right of it. The ball will go higher than before because a square club face has more loft than a closed one.

Ideally what you are trying to achieve is a shot that starts just a little right of target and then draws back, since not only is this one of the most powerful shots in golf but if you can be reasonably certain that you can reproduce this shape, then the whole game becomes simpler as you can then disregard, to a great extent anyway, any hazards on the right-hand side of the course.

CHAPTER SEVENTEEN

The push

The push shot starts right of target and continues in that direction with no curve in the flight (Fig 2.5a). This is so close to being a good shot that you should not need to make too much adjustment for it to become so. To produce a push shot, the club head is swinging from in-to-out, i.e. from 4 to 10 o'clock, with the club face square to that direction.

First, check your aim; it could be that you are simply aiming further right than you thought. Also check that the ball position is not too far back in your stance as this will tend to send it to the right (see Fig 15.1).

Once you have confirmed that your set up is satisfactory, if the ball still flies to the right then you have a swing fault. You could still be swinging your arms too much to the inside on the backswing, so re-read the previous chapter which dealt with this at some length.

If you feel that your backswing is satisfactory, you could be blocking your left side on the through swing, which will prevent the club head from moving towards the target through impact. At the start of the downswing the left knee moves laterally towards the target and then, as the downswing progresses, the left side has to turn to the left to clear a passage for the arms (Fig 17.1). You may be exaggerating the lateral element and therefore be deficient on the turn. It is not correct to turn the left hip out of the way as the initial action of the downswing — this is inclined to spin the whole body, resulting in an out-to-in swing path, so do not convert from a 'blocker' to a 'spinner'. You should feel that, as your arms reach impact, your left hip is now turning out of the way. You may be able to achieve this best by swinging to the finish position where most of your weight is towards the left heel, as this will encourage you to turn through (Fig 9.4). Alternatively, feel that the right knee moves towards the left at impact, which pushes the left hip out of the way.

Often by moving too laterally towards the target you will get ahead of the ball, which can restrict hand action and may convert what would have been a gently drawing shot into a straight push. This sometimes happens if you try to hit the ball too hard. Try hitting some smooth three-

*Fig 17.1. As the club head
approaches impact the left
side is clearing so that
the hand and arms have a clear passage
and can gradually square the club face*

quarter shots, keeping your head more behind the ball at
impact. This will allow your left side to clear better and
thereby enable your hands and forearms to correctly
rotate slightly to the left through the impact zone in a
powerful free-wheeling action.

CHAPTER EIGHTEEN

The push slice

This shot is less common and is a result of an in-to-out swing path, with the club face open (Fig 2.5b). The line of the swing is more in the 4 to 10 o'clock direction, but the player has not managed to square the club face to that line at impact. This shot can be caused by having a very strong grip, i.e. both hands turned well to the right with four knuckles of the left hand showing when you hold the grip up in front of you. Whereas you might imagine that this type of grip would close the club face at impact, what it actually tends to do is to block the hand action completely so that at impact the heel of the left hand is moving towards the target (Fig 18.1). Because the hands are turned so far to the right in the first place, the club head goes back naturally on an inside path and the outcome is a shot that starts right and then turns right.

To correct this action, the grip must be adjusted since it is the root cause of the problem. Unfortunately, this process will feel neither comfortable nor natural, and initially the shots may not be very encouraging either, but stick with it if you want to improve. Move your hands to the left on the grip until you can see only two to two-and-a-half knuckles of the left hand, with the right hand more at the side of the shaft (Fig 14.2). You need to become aware of how your hands should be working through impact so, using a 6 iron, carry out the hand action exercise detailed in Chapter 6. It may be difficult for you at first to grow accustomed to rotating you hands so much to the left through impact since you have always led with the heel of the left hand. Indeed it may take considerable hard work before you can repeat the action consistently. To give you another swing thought while you practise this exercise, try to feel that the toe of the club is going to beat the heel of the club back to the ball — for that to happen, the hands and arms must rotate to the left.

Once you can hit the ball off a tee so that it does not curve excessively in either direction, you can concentrate on the swing path. Despite the grip change, it is more than likely that you will still swing the club head to the inside on the backswing but, hopefully now, not quite as inside as with the strong grip. Imagine the backswing path

Fig 18.1. With a very strong grip the heel of the left hand pulls towards the target at impact, leaving the club face open and the left side of the body fails to turn out of the way

initially to be towards 3 o'clock before it turns inside towards 4 o'clock.

You will then be able to swing the club back to the ball from a better line and feel that you are clearing the left hip to the left at the same time as your arms are swung towards the target. If you are someone who hits the right going right shot you may move laterally towards the target, so you should re-read Chapter 17 on the push shot, paying particular attention to the advice on the hip action from the start of the downswing. Once you start to square the club face, you will also find your shots going a little lower and further.

CHAPTER NINETEEN

The straight hook

Having now covered all the shots possible from an in-to-out swing path, the last curving shot is the one that starts towards the target and then curves to the left. In this instance the ball is struck from an in-to-in swing at the moment the club head is moving towards the target, but the face is closed at impact (Fig 2.2c).

It is possible that you are addressing the ball with the club face closed, so check whether this is the case before making any other adjustments. If all seems well with the club face alignment, then check your grip. It may reveal that the hands are turned a little too far to the right. Move them to the left so that the back of the left hand and palm of the right face more towards the target (Fig 14.2). This will enable you still to use the good hand action that you have developed but without closing the club face.

You will need to experiment to find exactly the right grip, but do so allowing yourself to swing aggressively through the ball. Do not stifle your hand and arm rotation to correct the hook — instead, see if a grip change will do the trick.

If your grip seems satisfactory, then you must have a swing fault. Your hand and arm action is too strong, which suggests that the left side might not be controlling things as it should. Make sure that as you start the downswing, you lead with the left arm, keeping the back of the hand facing in the same direction as it was at the top of the swing (Fig 19.1). If the right side becomes too dominant too early, the arms will begin rotating to the left which will cause the back of the left hand to face the target too soon, thus squaring the blade too early. Change direction in an unhurried manner and keep pulling with the left arm right through impact so that the right hand will square the club face at, rather than before, impact.

Chapters 9 and 17 detailed leg action and how the body should turn out of the way through the impact zone, so re-read Chapter 11 on the 'Pull Hook' contains a half swing exercise to help control hand and arm action, which you should practise.

Once you have turned your shot from an uncontrollable straight hook into a gently drawing shot, you may like to

78

Fig 19.1. As the downswing starts feel that the back of the left hand remains looking more skywards to prevent your arms rotating to the left too early

experiment a little more by putting the ball back in your stance, say a ball's width to begin with, and see if you can make the ball start just right of target and draw back. I stress that you need to rid yourself of the hook first, but you can benefit from your over-active hands when they have become more educated.

CHAPTER TWENTY

Practice tips

By now you will know more about your swing and how to correct your faults. Do not expect to fully remember and understand all you have read, especially if you have only just started playing. Refer back to the chapters that concern you when necessary and work on correcting your swing in an orderly fashion. Here are a few more tips:

1 If you have to alter your grip, make sure every shot you play from now onwards is with that new grip — do not be tempted into what felt comfortable but was wrong.

2 Regularly check your grip and set up in a mirror; it is easy to get into bad habits.

3 To be certain of your swing characteristics, hit your 9 iron, 4 iron and driver. The direction of the ball with the 9 iron will tell you the direction of your swing path. The 4 iron will indicate club face alignment by which way the ball curves. The driver will tell you that your swing is too steep if the ball goes very high, or too shallow if it flies very low.

4 To further check the swing path, hit through short rough and you can easily see the direction in which the club head has travelled.

5 Practise with a 5 or 6 iron to ingrain changes. You are making life more difficult if you use a 3 iron or driver all the time.

6 If your swing is flat, find a sidehill where the ball is below your feet and practise there. This will encourage a more upright arm swing and less of a shoulder turn. Also on a flat lie, hit some shots where the ball is sitting down in the grass (you may have to lightly tread on the ball) since this situation requires an upright swing.

7 If your swing is upright, practise from a sidehill where the ball is above your feet. This will make your arms and body swing more horizontally, flattening the swing. On a flat lie set the ball on a fairly high tee peg and, using a driver, hit the ball but leave the tee peg in the ground. It is only with a flattish swing that this result is possible.